RCL Ø 2007
BIP Active Record 2010
pa. in
BIP 11/92
6.95

P9-DWF-569

music improvisation
as a classroom method

music
improvisation
as a classroom method

BERT KONOWITZ

A NEW APPROACH TO TEACHING MUSIC

Copyright ©1973 by Alfred Publishing Co., Inc.

All rights reserved. No part of this book may be reproduced or transmitted by any means, electronic or mechanical, including photocopying, recording, or by any information storage and retrieval system, without permission in writing from the Publisher.

ISBN: 0-88284-003-7

Library of Congress Catalog Number: 72-96015

Printed in the United States of America

Dedicated to Professors Mary and Catherine English
and the Potsdam Community

Special thanks to Professor Brock McElheran

WITHDRAWN

742075

CONTENTS

Introduction

Improvisation is generally considered as a technique associated solely with organ performance in the 16th and 17th centuries and contemporary jazz rock music. This misconception, which along with the idea that the ability to improvise is innate and predicated on the ability to skillfully perform on a musical instrument, has so successfully dwarfed the utilization of improvisational experience in music education as to mandate this text.

Improvisation is the spontaneous act of organizing, varying, creating, and performing. For the most part, teachers have thought of improvisation as a specialized musical skill requiring a unique background and/or a very special set of skills. There is clear and overwhelming evidence that these attitudes are unfounded. Musical improvisation is not a mystical, inexplicable phenomenon reserved for an exclusive few. It is a technique of creation and performance which is developed as skills are reduced to seemingly second nature. You can learn to improvise on some musical "instrument" and subsequently teach the skills to your students, whatever their age, grade, or level. This text will aid you to do these things.

However, the scope of activities covered in this book is far beyond the sheer acquisition of musical skills. Improvisation is considered here as a significant tool for experimenting, probing, inquiring, and discovering. Improvisational experiences represent a way for the student to test complex ideas at the level at which he can perform, control, and evaluate. The Improvisational Method represents a means that enables teachers and students to simulate mature experiences normally reserved for stages of advanced instruction at the earliest moment of musical encounter. The joy of *making music* (that is, performing, conducting, composing, arranging, and improvising) should infuse every step of musical growth, from the most primitive utterances to highly skilled activity. The Improvisational Method demands this condition. The learning experience is clearly structured in a sequential manner, and is developed as follows:

1. Begin by creating with the skills and perceptions that the student possesses, however basic they might be. (Phase I)

2. Expand basic skills and perceptions through improvisational experimentation. (Phase II)

3. Develop skills that afford greater performance capability and self-motivating inquiry. (Phase III)

In this way, every student becomes a performer, conductor, composer, arranger, and improvisor. If this seems too extravagant a claim for you, then it is suggested that you thoroughly digest every bit of material in this text, take a deep breath, and start developing an environment for experiencing and learning in the classroom that is dynamic, exciting, and believable for students living in our modern American society.

As the teacher, your path will be made easier by designing a two-part self-training program:

1. Learn and understand the basic nature and capability of the basic improvisation skills.

2. Explore and expand the many relationships that exist between the techniques and materials that you are already familiar with and the new ideas and approaches which you will encounter in this text.

It might well be that the benefits of improvisational experience go beyond the goals normally established in a music instruction text. The demands of a constantly changing society in the daily life of every citizen suggest that adjustment, even survival, is increasingly dependent on the ability of the individual to be flexible, adaptive, and spontaneous. Thus the rewards of improvisational experience as part of a human and aesthetic process appear significant enough to consider *improvisation as a classroom method.*

Organization and Use of This Book

This text is built around three "Creativity Sources":

Voice

Instruments

Keyboard

Each of these creativity sources is developed in three phases. They are:

Phase I—exploratory activity. This is the "tuning-up," "loosening-up" stage, when teacher and students freely explore and experiment through improvisation.

Phase II—expanding skill activities. Here, teacher and students elaborate on initial improvisational experiences through the increasing acquisition and development of musical skills.

Phase III—development and involvement. This is an expansion stage, in which prior improvisational experience is developed into an extended range of musical experience commonly associated with traditional patterns of inquiry found in "general music" and some performance programs.

Several operational plans may be used with these phases. Some teachers will choose to explore all of the Creativity Sources of Phase I, then the Creativity Sources of Phase II, and finally all the Creativity Sources of Phase III. Others may wish to explore one Creativity Source through all three phases before proceeding to the next Creativity Source. Still others might wish to alternate between various phases and/or activities to meet the needs of their individual classroom situations. Some classroom teachers with limited musical backgrounds may wish to limit their activities to the types suggested in Phase I and the beginning of Phase II. All of these approaches represent valid experiences and approaches, depending on individual teacher and student needs.

This book places heavy emphasis on encouraging the student to express his feelings, feelings which the author considers as universal as musical expression itself. The teacher's dialogue (T) and the students' responses (S) are considered "typical" (that is, average), similar to the type the author has encountered in countless classrooms over a period of many years. It is not intended that the teacher use the dialogues as a script, but that the dialogues be considered as one way of discovering the thrill of musical experience through improvisation. If the tactics found in this book are appropriate to your own teaching situation, then the material may be used intact. In many instances, however, a given technique will need to be altered to meet a specific, individual learning environment. These alterations may refer to grade level, age, or emotional and physical maturity. The teacher is encouraged to adapt his tactics according to the circumstances, even if completely new creative activities are subsequently developed. The more creative teacher will offer students greater latitude for individual growth.

A Sample Lesson Plan form is supplied at the end of each phase, for individual use and experimentation. The teacher is encouraged to complete a short lesson plan for each Creativity Source within a phase, and then to design various combinations of Creativity Sources. All lessons should be carefully planned, with emphasis on alternative tactics, in case those prepared fail to achieve the anticipated goal.

It is suggested that the following materials be considered basic classroom equipment:
   a) a piano (or any other keyboard instrument)
   b) environmental and manufactured instruments
   c) a tape recorder; students should consistently be encouraged to record their work, followed by critical analysis and discussion
   d) recordings and/or tapes; the selections should reflect a variety of styles, eras, and media
   e) overhead projector, blank transparencies, and necessary writing tools
   f) music manuscript book (which each student should own)
   g) a cardboard or plastic keyboard for each child

Phase I: EXPLORATORY ACTIVITIES

Beginning an activity—"tuning up"—is always difficult, whether one is writing a speech or story, cooking a new recipe, or composing a musical work. Most students feel hesitant, even foolish, about improvising. Therefore, the teacher should keep three important guides in mind:

1. Begin by involving the entire class. Students will become increasingly receptive if they are not exposed individually.
2. Every contribution made by students should be accepted without critical or evaluative judgment at this time. Support them, encourage them, involve them (and yourself).
3. Give very specific directions. Make verbal directions short, succinct, and sure. When directing the entire class in improvisational responses, use your hands in the same manner that the conductor of a vocal or instrumental group does, thus reducing the need for verbalization.

Here are some suggestions for basic conducting:

a) to get louder (forte), raise palms upward;
   to get softer (piano), move palms downward.
b) to get higher, raise arms in a sweeping gesture;
   to get lower, lower arms in a sweeping gesture.
c) to get faster, quickly make small circles;
   to get slower, slowly make small circles.
d) to create a very short (staccato) effect, make short chops;
   to create a very smooth (legato) effect, gently make undulating lines.

Creativity Source-*Voice*

Strategy: To initiate improvisation by "loosening" everybody up by focusing on expressing feelings through vocal sounds.

Tactics:

Teacher(T): (happy) "Good morning boys and girls!"
"I wonder how you would greet me if I told you that today was the last day of school?"
Students(S): (s h o u t e d) "GOOD MORNING, DOCTOR KONOWITZ!"
(T): (sad) "How would you say that if I told you there was school Saturday?"
(S): (mumbled) "good morning doctor konowitz."

Strategy: Through speech patterns, explore the basic concepts of music such as dynamics (soft-loud), tempo (slow-fast), and pitch (high-low).

Tactics:

(T) (softly) "We're pleased to have Martha Langer, a new girl, in our class. Keep repeating her name as I suggest different moods to you."
(S) "Mar-tha Lang-er, Mar-tha Lang-er . . . " (keep repeating)
(T) (as students continue repeating name) "Say it the way you feel when you're lonely . . . bored."
(S) Students respond.
(T) (loudly) "When you're happy—as happy as we all are to have Martha with us."
(S) Students respond.
(T) (slow tempo) "Like a turtle walks . . . like you're tired."
(S) Students respond.
(T) (fast tempo) "Like you're a hurricane . . . like running for the bus."

6

(S)	Students respond.
(T)	(low pitch) "Like you've sunk to the bottom of the sea."
(S)	Students respond.
(T)	"Good! Whenever I point to the tip of my nose with my right index finger, improvise. Now, as I point to you, improvise on your name by varying the dynamics . . . tempo . . . and pitch."
(S)	Students say their own names many times as they vary the dynamics, tempo, and pitch.
(T)	"Now, make a sound on the last syllable of Martha Langer's name."
(S)	Students make the sound errrrrrrrrrrr.
(T)	"Using that sound, change the pitch as I raise and lower my arm."

(S)	Students respond.
(T)	"Now let's have some of you conduct. Be sure to make your directions very clear as you ask us to improvise on your idea. When you have finished practicing in your groups, each one of you will perform the improvisation before the class. After performing it twice, you will all return to your groups and make any adjustments that you feel are necessary. Then we will tape record the improvisations and listen to them."

Enrichment Activities

1. Distribute, or have students bring, newspapers to class. First, all students read aloud from their newspapers. Naturally, the results appear chaotic. Then direct students to read their specific selections aloud as they change the pitch of their voices and vary the dynamics, tempo, accents, and phrasing appropriate to the mood. Finally, have students come before the class to conduct an improvisation. Through this experience, the students are learning to conduct, compose, perform, and improvise while using minimal skill material.

2. Select a name—a student, teacher, principal, celebrity, etc. Ask the entire class to say the name in a variety of ways. Then divide the class into two parts. Part one says the name as a rhythmic ostinato; part two improvises on the name. Begin by having the class say the name so as to express the way they feel about that person, the way the name makes them feel in different situations. Here is an example:

Say "Louis Armstrong" softly, keep repeating.

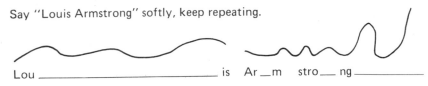

Lou _____ is Ar __m   stro__ ng _____

3. Select various objects that have characteristic sounds (refrigerator, jet plane, various machines, purring of a kitten, static on the radio, etc.). First, have students experiment with the object word (jet plane, etc.). Then conduct them in an improvisation, including the way it sounds to them, the way they feel about that particular object, and/or the way they wish the object sounded. Experiment by dividing the class in two for an improvisation in the manner described in number 2 above. Finally, have students serve as conductors.

4. Create your own improvisational experiences, using vocal sounds as the Creativity Source.

5. Read Bert Konowitz, *Vocal Improvisational Method,** for further activities.

6. Perform *Zodiac: A Vocal Improvisation Encounter.* * This is a two-part vocal composition which offers considerable opportunity for the aforementioned type of vocal improvisational activity.

.

*All references bearing an asterisk are available from Alfred Publishing Co., Inc., Port Washington, N.Y.

Creativity Source-*Instruments*

"Instruments (from L. *instruere;* cf. instruction); the generic name for all mechanisms producing musical sounds; hence for all musical media with the exception of the human voice."*

The use of the term *instrument* in this section refers to the broad definition given above. Thus, instruments are divided into several categories, which include the body, environmental instruments, manufactured or orchestral instruments, and electronic media. The sound capability of each category includes:

BODY   *mouth:*   "tch tch" sound (made by putting the tip of the tongue against the teeth, pulling in the lower lip behind the upper teeth, and inhaling a long, sustained breath), kissing sound, whistle, whistle position of lips, but inhaling, throat sounds including growl, clearing of throat, cough, etc.

              hands: rubbing palms together, finger snaps, hand-clapping, nail-clicking, squeezing palms together while clasping fingers, slapping various parts of the body with the hands, etc.

              feet: feet scraping and/or sliding against floor, tapping of heel or toe of shoe on the floor, hitting heels. together, hitting objects with feet, etc.

ENVIRONMENTAL   metallic objects in a jar or container (nails, clips, tacks, cereal, pennies), cellophane or soft plastic, cereal boxes (including rice, beans, spaghetti), toy instruments, empty or liquid-filled bottles or glasses, metal pipe shafts, eating utensils, anything.

*Willie Apel, Harvard Dictionary of Music, Cambridge, Mass. : Harvard University Press, 1965, p. 355.

MANUFACTURED ORCHESTRAL	percussion (drums, wood-blocks, cymbals, triangles, tambourines, claves, bongos, bells, gongs, etc.), strings (violin, viola, cello, bass, auto-harp, guitar, etc.), woodwinds (oboe, clarinet, bassoon, flute, saxophone, kazoo, tonette, flutophone, melodica, etc.); brass (trumpet, trombone, tuba, etc.).

The tactics below are related to clapping. Any of the sound sources indicated under the Body, Environmental, or Manufactured sections may be used in the same way.

Strategy: To initiate improvisation by uncovering the multiple ways that the full palette of instrumental colors (body, environmental, manufactured) may be used in expressing feelings.

Tactics:

(T) "Using only your hands, create an angry sound."

(S) Students rub hands together roughly and quickly, some smack hands together, etc.

(T) "Now create a gentle sound . . . happy . . . frightened."

(S) Students give varied responses.

(T) "I would like you to repeat exactly what you hear. I will clap a 2-measure question . . . all of you clap back exactly what you hear. Exact answers are called *parallel answers*."

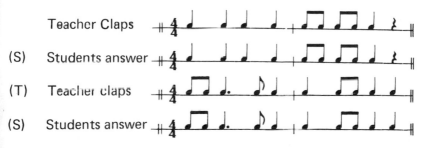

Strategy: To explore the basic concept of dynamics, accents, phrasing, and tempo through instrumental sounds.

Tactics:

(T)   "Good! Let's try a few more." Teacher claps a few more, making each one just a little more rhythmically complex and using different dynamics, accents, phrasing, and tempos. Here are some examples:

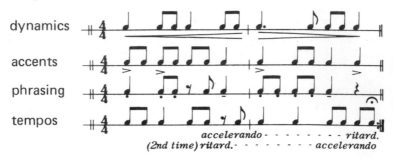

(S)   Students answer with parallel answers.

(T)   "Now, let's have some of you clap a question as we all give parallel answers." Individual students are selected to give the questions. The pace of the class should be active and dynamic.

(S)   Students engage in questions and parallel answers, using a variety of musical concepts.

(T)   "Now I would like you to clap an answer to my question which has a slightly different rhythm. These answers are called *contrasting answers.* Be sure that they are only two measures long."

(T)   Claps question

(S)   Students answer

(T)   Claps several more questions, varying their rhythm, dynamics, accents, phrasing, tempo, emotion, and character.

(S)   Students answer with 2-measure, contrasting answers.

12

(T)   "Now, after you reply to my question with a 2-measure contrasting answer, continue clapping as you vary *any* of the ingredients we have been working with."

(T)   Claps

(S)   Students clap a long contrasting answer. They are actually performing an "improvisation," as some redesign of the original idea has now occurred.

Examples of a possible improvised response:

After considerable experimentation by the class, the teacher will aid the students in combining different instrumental sound sources. The class might be divided first into two sections, each with its respective instrumental sound. Later, a class may be divided into several smaller groups, each with a different instrument.

Enrichment Activities

1. Create a "discovery center" in the classroom by designating a particular space (window sill, closet, shelf) where students will put environmental instruments that they bring to class. Students should be encouraged to make their own instruments. Instrument-making can be a cooperative project between the music teacher and the art or industrial arts teacher.

2. Instrumental improvisations may be suggested by various motivational aids. Programmatic devices suggest stories, situations, and scenes. Hold up a poster, picture, or photograph and ask the students to use their instruments in an improvisation which re-creates the suggested scene. Students may be encouraged to write their own stories, which will be read aloud and musically re-created through instrumental improvisation. Many creative experiences in this area can be fostered through a cooperative effort between the music teacher and the English, social studies, language, or math teachers.

In addition, emotion-laden devices can be used as motivating aids. Responses based on feelings and sensations may be provoked by a tree leaf, a picture of water, the sound of thunder, the sight of the sun at its various stages, and other articles of nature. Articles of texture (wool, cloth, a towel, silk, sandpaper, a paper bag, sand) may provide additional stimuli. It is probably obvious that a joint venture between the music teacher and art teacher is desirable.

3. Choose a manufactured instrument and create an improvisation by using the instrument in an unusual way. (Playing a violin with the back of the bow, rubbing a violin bow along the edge of a cymbal, playing a woodwind or brass instrument into some type of resonating chamber such as a closet, drawer, or corner).

4. Create an improvisation by combining vocal and instrumental sounds.

Creativity Source-*Keyboard*

The use of keyboard instruments is often limited to "piano lessons." In the tactics described below, we are assuming that the student has had *no,* or at best, minimal, experience. For the teacher, only very basic keyboard experience is required. The term keyboard, as used here, includes a broad range of keyboard and keyboard percussion instruments such as piano, organ, electric piano, electric organ, bell-like or celeste-type instruments, or even a harpsichord, which many older students can construct from a kit.

The only conditions necessary for initiating keyboard experience are:

1. One piano, though more are helpful. Each student should have a cardboard (or plastic) keyboard on his desk.

2. A well-defined traffic pattern should be established so that students may move to and from the piano with maximum case and speed.

Here is a suggested pattern:

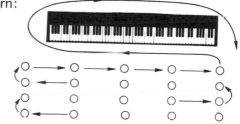

Strategy: To initiate improvisation by discovering the accessibility of keyboard instruments for the non-performer as a means of expressing one's feelings.

Tactics: Assign each row in the class a number (Row #1, 2). Select one student in each row as a row leader. The row leader's responsibility is to make sure that his row gets to the piano and back effortlessly. From one to four students at a time may play. Because many students feel that they do not possess the necessary skill to make any contribution at the piano, the teacher should take extra care to be supportive and encouraging. Such phrases as "very original," "that was an interesting idea," "very adventurous," "that had lots of activity," should be used. Defer value judgments such as "good," "bad," "why didn't you?". If the student does not play at all, gently exhort him to at least make an attempt.

Students will simulate playing the piano at their desk keyboards until it is their turn to go to the piano.

(T)   "Row 1, please stand. Come to the front of the room and form a line next to the piano, facing me. Using only the *white notes,* any white notes, create a sound that reflects the way you feel when you are hungry."

(S)   Students make rumbling, dissonant sounds.

(T)   "Still using the white notes, create a sound that is sad . . . sleepy . . . energetic . . . lonely . . . loving . . . like rain . . . like the way you feel about school . . . about your friends . . . about your teacher . . . about yourself."

(S)   Students respond in various ways. (The teacher should frequently change the rows that are improvising, to give everyone an equal chance and to keep the pace of the class moving dynamically.)

(T)   Now, using any black notes, suggest more vivid imagery that will serve as a basis for student keyboard improvisation.

(S)   Students respond with black-note improvisations using only black notes.

(T)   "Again using only the black notes, I would like you to add the use of the sustaining pedal (the pedal on the far right) by either keeping it down, or experimenting in any way you like. With that in mind, improvise on the picture of a space rocket taking off and traveling into outer space . . . being on the bottom of the ocean . . . being lost in a maze . . . a stream flowing down the mountain, growing larger, finally reaching a great expanse of water."

(S)   Students respond with varied black-note improvisations.

(T)　"How many of you have been to a parade? How do you feel at a parade?"

(S)　"Excited," "happy," "tired," and so forth.

(T)　"Playing only on the black notes, express your feelings about what you see and hear at a parade." The teacher should play this repetitive drone bass:

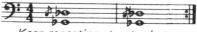

Keep repeating at a steady tempo

(T)　Encourage students to experiment in different registers of the piano by suggesting different sounds and sights at a parade, such as piccolos, tubas, lots of people, or the converging sounds of bands. Ask the last student in line to get softer and softer until the "activity" fades away, then begin by playing the following "Western Bass":

Keep repeating

"Does this bass give you a mental picture of the West? Using only the black notes, describe your feelings about the West."

(S)　Students respond with black-note improvisations.

(T)　After many students have played, you might change the scenario by playing the following Indian bass:

Keep repeating

(T)　"Here we are at an Indian reservation. Create improvisations describing Indian dances, ceremonies, meetings, and customs."

(S)　Students improvise on black keys.

Strategy: To explore the basic concepts of dynamics, accents, phrasing, and tempo through keyboard experience.

Tactics:

(T)   "Find the white note located between the group of two black notes. It is called *D*. I will play a question and you respond on that note with a parallel answer."

Teacher: Question   Students: Answer

"Now I will play the same question as before. While it has the same rhythm, something about it is slightly different. Listen, then play a parallel answer, making sure that you include the new element."

(T) (S)

(T)   "I will now play the same question again, and you play a contrasting answer, changing only the element being stressed and *not* the rhythm."

(T) (S)

After this question has been used, the teacher should create several more with new rhythms and notes before proceeding to the next group. This routine should be followed through the above sequence. Here are some sample questions and responses:

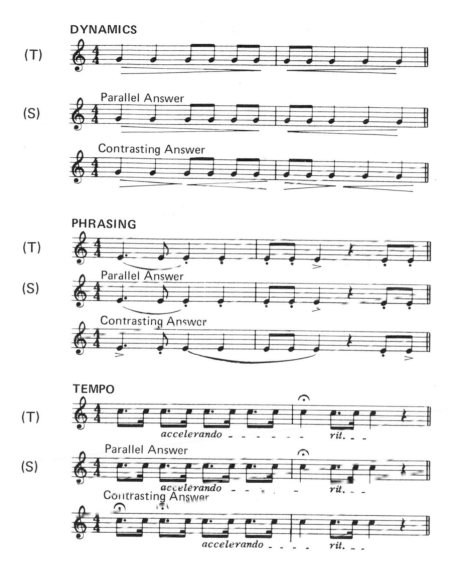

During these activities, all of the students should have one or more turns at the piano. Now two rows are formed, one on the right side of the keyboard, and the other on the left side.

"ON DECK"   PLAYER PLAYER   "ON DECK"

The objective is to foster student-directed creative experiences through improvisation. This experience will strengthen the student's ear training as well as his rhythm and pitch development.

Each student on the left plays a question to the student on the right. The emphasis will be on changes in dynamics, accents, phrasing, and tempo. The student on the right replies with a parallel answer, waits for a restatement of the question, and then gives a contrasting answer. When the students have finished, both the treble and bass row students return to their seats. Then two more rows form at the piano. After the entire class has finished this exercise, begin again by switching the rows (those that played treble now play bass, and vice versa). Encourage students to use many different tones and registers in their questions. Activity should be fast paced, so that the students do not remain at their seats too long. All seated students should be simulating playing questions and answers at their desk keyboards.

Enrichment Activities

1. Develop improvisational activity through the use of tone cluster, that is, closely spaced grouping of tones. For example:

Ask the students to group two or more tones together to achieve a specific sound quality. Many programmatic devices may be used to stimulate this activity. Showing pictures or drawings, or reading something aloud while the student creates an improvisation with tone clusters, is an effective tactic. Students may be encouraged to use large groupings of tones, which might be played with the palm, forearm, entire arm, or back of the hand. Students often confuse the use of unfamiliar techniques with chaos and disorder. By stressing careful use of dynamics, performances will reflect a better-defined sense of self-discipline. Abundant use of the sustaining right pedal often adds a colorful richness to the improvisations.

2. The *telephone conversation:* Since the telephone figures so largely in the lives of most students, the dialogue question-and-answer technique may be used to achieve extended keyboard activity. Have two students at a time go to the piano to play, using either random tones (white or black notes) or specific individual tones in the manner they would normally speak on the telephone. Thus they will be using rhythms, pitches, dynamics, phrasing, and tempo to reflect what they would normally say through speech. Various humorous situations might be developed by suggesting specific scenes (talking to mother, to friends, to a prospective employer, the police station, the principal).

3. Encourage the students to use their exposure to media (television, movies, radio, printed matter) as a framework for developing background improvisations at the piano. Music for commercials, stories, and scenes, as a background for a narrative reading, offers many creative possibilities to the student.

Synthesis of Phase I

The activities experienced thus far will serve to promote the following:

Self-revelation: "I *CAN* improvise" (everybody can). "I can be spontaneous, creative . . . *I can make music!"*

Group identification: "I can function, perform, create, improvise, learn from and with others."

Motivation: "My superficial experiences with a wide range of improvisational experiences has aroused my interest in extending my skills in creating for voices, piano, instruments, groups; in writing stories and setting them to music, creating sound collages, in writing a score that can be performed by others; in expanding my experience with what I am learning in social studies, English, art, shop, and language by incorporating them into a musical composition that I can create and perform with others; in learning how to use musical Creativity Sources that are continually around me, in spite of my performance limitations."

The activities in the Creativity Sources explored in Phase I should be combined at some point, so that creations and performance reflect how voices and instruments, piano and voices, instruments and piano, piano and instruments and voices can be interrelated in an improvisational setting. Phase I is a "getting started" stage and should not be necessarily evaluated for the quality of the product. The emphasis is on *PROCESS,* on doing and experiencing—on *beginning!*

Phase II represents an extension, strengthening, refinement, and development of musical activities begun in Phase I. The goals of Phase II are:

Explore in depth the potential for creative growth through improvisation, using the Creativity Sources of voice, instrument, and keyboard. The activities will include performance, composition, conducting, singing, and improvisation.

Develop skills, which include vocal, instrumental, and keyboard "performance," composition, singing, conducting, recording, and improvising.

Expand upon the relationship between classroom experiences and the professional world of music. This will include research through reading, listening to music, writing, and a broad range of experimental activities.

LESSON PLAN FORM

CREATIVITY SOURCE

Class:

Date:

Phase	Strategy	Tactics	Materials (if any)	Alternative Tactics
I	1.	1.	1.	1.

Phase II: EXPERIENTIAL ACTIVITIES

The focus of Phase II is on individual and group involvement through skill-evolving activities. Phase II is an outgrowth of the tactics begun in Phase I. Its activities begin where Phase I left off. In most cases, Phase I requires only a short amount of time, possibly from one to four classes. Much more time will be spent in Phases II and III.

Creativity Source-*Voice*

Strategy: to develop student responsibility for organizing and creating with the concepts of music through vocal experiences.

Tactics:

(T) "Choose some word, object phrase, or subject that you might see or hear in this room such as . . ."

(S) "Exit . . . Quiet! . . . Peace . . . . Now really boys and girls!"

(T) "Good! Let's divide into six small groups. Each member of the group will get a chance to create an improvisation on his idea (motif). By using your hands and arms to conduct, you can lead your group in an interesting, spoken improvisation by varying dynamics, tempo, and pitch."

(S) "How about backwards, like 'tixe' for 'exit'?"

(T) "Good!" That's called *retrograde motion,* the backward reading of a musical idea.

(S) "Or quai—eh—h—h—t for 'quiet'?"

(T) "Excellent! That's called *augmentation.* In music, augmentation is doubling the rhythmic value of a tone. Okay, off to work."

After considerable time spent in this activity, the class reconvenes. Each group performs and all performances are taped for later student evaluation. The class discovers other concepts in the improvisations—articulation (staccato, legato, portamento), phrasing (punctuation, emphases), timbre (varied sound qualities such as clapping hands over the mouth, speaking through a pinched nose or clenched teeth), and form (ABA, rondo type, rhapsody). Later on, these improvisations will be notated (using any type of symbol) on transparencies for class viewing and evaluation.

Strategy: To transfer creative insights gained in spoken activity to pitched activities.

Tactics:

(T) "Everyone hum a tone, any tone. Listen around the room and match your tone with others until it becomes one. (Pause) Good! Now create different timbres holding the same tone."

(S) Some open their mouths to make vowel sounds; others put their hands over their mouth to create varied effects.

(T) "Choosing any sound you like, change your note as my conducting changes." The teacher indicates changes in pitch by moving the arms up and down. In developing variations in pitch, the teacher indicates specific pitch changes to various students or small groups in the class. The emphasis is on variety of changing sounds.

(T) "Fine! Now, let's have some of you come up and create variations with the class."

(S) Student conductors experiment in creating variations with class, discovering that the group can be divided in parts to create *polyphony* (the simultaneous combining of several independent musical lines). Some improvisations may be developed which capture the emotional quality of such themes as "A Night on Bald Mountain" or "Anitra's Dance." Later on, the improvisations are compared to actual recordings of such works. Art stories, even newspaper headlines, may be catalysts for pitch improvisations.

Strategy: To organize chordal accompaniments as backgrounds for melodic improvisations.

Tactics:

(T)   With the class divided into low, middle, and high voices, the teacher strikes a tone (for example, *C*). The low voices sing *C*, the middles *E*, and the highs *G*. "That's called a I chord. All my instructions to you now will be with my hands. The raised left hand, with palm facing out, will tell you what chord to sing."

Teacher and class practice chords, using student conductors with large and small groups. Examples of chord combinations are: I IV V I; I V I; I IV I V I; I I IV IV V V I I. Chords are sung with varied dynamics, tempi, articulation, and tonal color. Eventually the students will learn many different ways to sing the chords, including (a) alberti, (b) waltz, (c) oom-pah, (d) broken chord, (e) jazz, and (f) rock basses. Here are examples:

(b) waltz

(c) oom-pah

(d) broken chord

(e) jazz

Bop da bop da (etc.)

(f) rock basses

For further examples of rock-jazz materials, see Bert Konowitz, *Vocal Improvisation Method.* *

Strategy: to explore specific melodic materials for improvisation.

Tactics:

(T)   "Melodies are developed from chords, using either scales or chord tones. My right hand indicates the melodic improvisational material to be used. *Scales* are indicated by the index finger of the right hand scratching cheek; *chord tones* by tugging the collar or tie with the right hand." Sing and conduct scales and chord tones as they relate to a given chord.

Improvising now includes alteration of the order, dynamics, rhythm, articulation, phrasing, or tonal color of the scale or chord tones. While most of the students softly sing an accompaniment on a given chord progression, individual students and/or small groups improvise melodies, using scale or chord tones. Later, additional melodic materials will be explored.

Strategy: To involve each student in the artistic decision-making processes while exploring musical concepts.

Tactics:

(T)   "Let's improvise our own musical compositions either as a large group or in smaller groups. These compositions will be performed in class. Then, each group presentation will be taped, analyzed, and evaluated. Later, performances for other classes, in assemblies and/or for parents, may take place. You might apply these techniques to musical compositions that specifically incorporate vocal improvisation, for example, 'Zodiac.' "

Through vocal improvisation, we have directly involved each student in the discovery of basic musical concepts, while he creates like a composer, conducts like a conductor, and improvises like everyone can and should!

Enrichment Activities

1. Small groups of students create Zodiac-type compositions. Various themes that offer multiple groupings, or sections, in a composition include: the seasons (4), days of the week (7), hours of a clock (12) or in a day (24), months in a year (12), meals in a day (3).

2. Have the students practice the skills of vocal improvisation, stressing execution of chords in varying patterns, as well as stressing accuracy and good choral tone in improvising with scales and chord tones. All students should be given as many opportunities as possible for conducting, with small groups and with the entire class.

3. Select song material from series text or sheet music. Ask the students to design appropriate accompaniment backgrounds through choral improvisation techniques. Then have student conductors lead the class in melodic improvisations based on the chord pattern of notated songs. Choose a variety of periods and styles, including *classic-romantic* (Alberti, block chord, broken chord bases) and *contemporary* (block chord, single note basses, including jazz-rock patterns). Ask the student to create improvisations in the style of Mozart, the Beatles, Bessie Smith. *This might well lead to the need for students to listen to the music of various composers and performers, which is the heart of the activity that will occur in Phase III.*

Creativity Source-*Instruments*

Strategy: To develop student reponsibility for organizing and creating with the concepts of music through instrumental experiences.

Tactics: (Environmental and traditional percussion instruments are distributed to students.)

(T) "Your instruments have specific capabilities, such as how loudly or softly they can be played. Everyone test his instrument to find out how softly and loudly it will play.

(S) Students play, creating noise and seeming chaos.

(T) "Now, some of you have instruments whose pitch is definite. Test your instrument to determine whether it is pitched or nonpitched." Students play, again creating noise and seeming chaos.

(T) "Some of you have instruments whose pitch can be altered. Experiment with yours and see if it is like that."

(S) Students experiment with instruments. Some find that variations in the amount of pressure applied to the surface of the instrument will affect the pitch. Other discoveries include the effect of loosening and tightening tuning pegs, and shortening or elongating an object, as well as the different sounds of various vibrating elements: glass, metal, water-filled glasses.

(T) "Let's develop an improvisation that emphasizes variation in pitch. Select a word that describes a feeling, like 'love,' 'fear,' anger,' 'sadness.' Using the blank overhead transparency that I will give you, notate a guide, or score for an instrumental improvisation based on the emotion that you have selected. If you have difficulty getting started, use some of the techniques we used in our earlier improvisations (Phase I). Do you remember any?"

(S) "Questions and answers, both parallel and contrasting," "random sounds that create the actual sound quality of a word," "we could start with one rhythm and then add different rhythms," "we could use different phrasing, tempo, accents, dynamics."

(T) Divide the class into groups of about five each. The students should be encouraged to work as quietly as possible, so that they may give careful attention to their projects. During this period, the teacher moves around the room answering questions and raising questions that will require the students to experiment and develop new directions. Some time might be devoted to having the entire class suggest notational systems. If your students do not have adequate notational skills, a "functional" notation system should be encouraged. Thus a score might appear as follows:

Emotion: "love"

drum	/ / / /	
triangle	/ / / /	Keep repeating
ratchet		～～～～～
box of tacks shake **5 seconds** (soft)	rest	shake
glasses		/ rest / rest

(S) After a suitable amount of time has passed (15 minutes, 3 classes, a week, 2 weeks) the students present their compositions. Each group will have a conductor. The class may follow the score which is on the transparency, now placed on the overhead projector. After a taped performance is made, the class listens to the recording and evaluates it in terms of: the relationship of the musical product to the emotion being described musically; what part pitch variation had in the success or lack of success of the performance; what effect dynamics, phrasing, tempo, accents, and rhythmic change had. Did the performance reflect creativity, originality, spontaneity? Was the conductor clear in giving directions? Was the score clearly notated, the players cohesive in their performance, etc.?

(T) Similar tactics may be used in experimenting with timbre (the tone qualities of instruments). Student performances might be motivated by techniques that gradually include specific musical techniques such as a fast, roaring train or plane sound, the sound or feeling of rain bouncing off a tin roof, the picture of a remote castle, high on a mountain, barely visible through the mist, and so on.

Strategy: To organize chordal accompaniments as backgrounds for melodic improvisations.

Tactics: With the class divided into instrumental choirs and grouped by instrument (woodwinds, brass, strings, metal, glass, etc.) or pitch range (low, middle, high), the teacher strikes a tone—for example, *C.* Continue to follow the procedures suggested in the Synthesis section of Phase I. Be sure to substitute the word "instruments" for "voices." These tactics are also suitable for instrumental exploration and may be carried through the *Strategies* restated here:

Strategy: To explore specific melodic materials for improvisation.
Strategy: To involve each student in the artistic decision-making processes while exploring musical concepts.

For project presentation and evaluative techniques, follow the suggested procedures found on page 25, under (T) heading. *Experimentation* and *development* should be the keys in Phase II. Instrumental improvisation and compositions should reflect a combination of nonpitched, fixed, and variable-pitch instruments. The teacher and the students are encouraged to experiment with electronic devices, including tape recorders (variable speeds, playing tape backwards, and splicing), tape loops, and radios (white noise). (See Walter Sear, *The New World of Electronic Music.) *

Enrichment Activities

1. Write original verses. Read them aloud and create instrumental improvisations around them. Then compose an improvisational composition, orchestrate with instruments, and perform, tape, and evaluate.

2. Use multimedia material to serve as the theme of an accompaniment to an improvised instrumental performance. Slides, movies (prepared or student-made), flashing lights (strobe, multi-circuit), varying reflective objects (prisms, mirrors), and flashlights with colored gelatins can be used to create original multi-media shows.

3. Create an improvised instrumental performance reflecting different eras and styles of music, including rock, the Berlioz orchestra, the Haydn string quartet. These activities will create the need for additional information, requiring the students to make explorations through listening to records, reading, and research. These tactics are the essence of the activities found in Phase III.

Creativity Source-*Keyboard*

Strategy: To develop student capabilities for organizing and manipulating the concepts of music through keyboard experience.

Tactics: The sequence of activities will be from *emotional* (involving feelings) to *programmatic* (scenes and stories) to *musical* (dealing with musical concepts such as rhythm, silence, high-low, piano, etc.).

Emotional

(T)   "Now class, I would like for each row to come to the piano. When you do, create an improvisation by using only the white notes, as you express a specific mood for feeling. I can understand that you might feel silly doing this because some of you are not pianists, but the really important thing to keep in mind is how closely your improvisation comes to expressing your message."

(S)   Students line up at the piano. Unlike the experience in Phase I, in which students created "sounds" to describe feelings, each student sits at the piano for his turn. Some students will be very reluctant or even appear unable to do this. They should be encouraged to begin by playing one note, then playing it softer, louder, faster, slower; then two notes, louder, slower, higher, lower; then change it around—play several notes in varying order, higher, lower, angry, peaceful, gentle; then the way the student feels about the piano, the way he feels in general, and so on. *When difficulty arises in initiating a task, return to the lowest possible level of the activity, so that the student has an opportunity to develop a sense of sureness and safety by working within an evolving structure.*

(T)   Many emotions will be improvised on. Students might give each other a specific emotion to improvise on, with the teacher directing evaluations of the effectiveness of different musical elements in achieving a desired effect.

Programmatic

(T)   "In the next set of improvisations, two of you will sit down at the keyboard. Select a particular scene, picture, story, or situation and create an improvisation together which describes the idea you have in mind."

(S)   Students improvise in twos, possibly threes, dealing with such subjects as a marching band, a machine with many gears, an elephant, thunder, a locomotive picking up speed. Students should be rotated often, so that each one has at least one turn.

Musical

(T)   "Let's create improvised performances with new ideas.

What are some of the components of a musical composition?"

(S) "Movement, relaxation, silence, sound, high-low, loud-soft, beat-no beat."

(T) "Good! Using any one of these concepts, create a score for three people to play at the piano. Each of you might want to take a specific range to play within, or even specific notes. If you have no experience in writing music, use the functional notation system." The class should now be divided into small composition groups away from the piano. When the scores are ready, each group performs and then is evaluated.

Strategy: To organize accompaniment patterns as structures for melodic improvisations.

Tactics: The sequence of experiences will be: single notes, harmonic intervals (two tones struck together), and triads (three-tone chords).

Single Notes

(T) "Notice that the keyboard is organized by groups of two and three black notes. The white note to the left of the two black notes is *C*. Play it. Now locate *F* and *G*. Each time you see a I symbol, play *C*. When you see a IV, play *F* and when you see a V, play *G*. First, I will call them out loud. Third row come up to the piano, please. I would like four of you standing at the piano at one time. With your left hand, play a I."

(S) Students will have difficulty finding the notes, but should continue to make the effort.

(T) Write the following harmonic pattern on the board as students write it in their manuscript books.

I I I I IV IV IV IV V V V V I I I I
Other patterns might be:
I I V V IV V I I I IV V I I V V I

Students should be encouraged to create their own harmonic patterns.

Harmonic Intervals and Triads

These activities will be used by those students who already have keyboard experience, or as a guide for extending the tactics already encountered beyond single notes.

(T)   Follow similar procedures for locating harmonic intervals and triads, as were used in the tactics for single notes. Here are some basses that classes, depending on their skill, might explore:

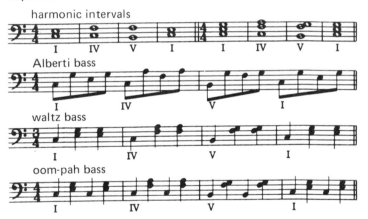

Strategy: To explore specific melodic materials for improvisation.

Tactics: The sequence of activity is from tetrachords to scales to modes (Dorian and Mixolydian).

Scales

(T)   "Place the five fingers of your right hand on any five consecutive keys, black or white. Improvise on these five notes, playing them in any order, rhythm, tempo, or level of dynamics. Now place your hands so that they look like this (a cardboard keyboard, thumbtacked above the front blackboard should be used by the teacher to demonstrate finger positions):

As I play a repetitive tone in the bass (to keep a feeling of continuity), play the tones in this C major scale, in any order, rhythm, tempo, or dynamic."

(S)   Though initial efforts are cautious, practice will result in a passage similar to the one below:

(T)   Experiment by having the student place his hands on tetrachords, beginning from various notes. More experienced students should at first be encouraged to use one hand, then both, for scale improvisations. As students demonstrate increasing facility, they should be encouraged to perform improvisations using both hands. This will require increasing skill.

As students display greater facility, relate the scale-type improvisation to a specific harmonic pattern. This tactic may be accomplished as follows:

(T)   "Now class, form two lines at the keyboard. The student on the left will perform the harmonic accompaniment by using one of the basses that you can play. The one on the right will improvise with the appropriate scale, beginning his scale on the tone that corresponds to the chord his partner is playing."

(S)   Here is an example:

(T) Students are now encouraged to design scores, indicating a treble and bass part, with instructions for the harmonic pattern and scales to be used.

(S) Here is one score:

Improvise with ♩ ♫ ♩ rhythm in right hand.

	C scale	G scale	F scale	G scale	C scale	F scale	G scale	C scale

Waltz bass: I   V   IV   V   I   IV   V   I

(T) Write the Dorian and Mixolydian modes on the blackboard. The Dorian resembles a Major scale, but the third and seventh steps are lowered. The Mixolydian contains only a lowered seventh step of the scale. Dorian and Mixolydian modes can be created from any starting tone, as long as the characteristic tones are altered.

Dorian mode   Mixolydian mode
1 2 3 4 5 6 7 8   1 2 3 4 5 6 7 8

(S) Students write tones in their manuscript books. Increasing emphasis will be placed on reading music and on notation.

(T) "Follow the procedures similar to those used in scale tactics." Once students become skillful with the Mixolydian mode, have them use it when improvising on a V chord. Indicated below are several sample basses:

"D" Dorian

"G" Mixolydian

Strategy: To involve each student in the artistic decision-making process while exploring musical concepts.

Students will be encouraged to write musical compositions, using various bass patterns and melodic techniques. While beginning with functional notation, the increasing emphasis the teacher places on standard notation activity will increase music reading and writing skills. Various "emotional," "programmatic," and/or "musical" ideas should be used as structuring and motivating devices. Written compositions should include sections that offer the freedom to improvise. Solo, duet, trios, or even quartet pieces combining keyboard and other instruments will be created. Students might also be encouraged to combine vocal and instrumental activities in their keyboard experiences.

Enrichment Activities

1. Considerable interest in Indian music, instruments, and performers has been demonstrated in America during the last decade. The use of Hindu modes, called *ragas,* is an attractive device for developing musicianship through improvisation. As the teacher plays a repetitive C in the bass register, students will improvise on any combination of tones found in the following suggested ragas:

Bahirava

Moduvanti (associated with the sultriness of the Indian afternoon)

2. Create jazz-rock style improvisations by accenting the tones in the scales and modes on the second and fourth beat. The teacher or the more advanced students may play the following basses:

Jazz—walking bass

Rock—bass

3. Use improvised/notated keyboard experiences in relation to student-created dramatic activities (creating a "show," a TV commercial, background for original poetry or prose, etc.).

Synthesis of Phase II

The activities of Phase II will serve to produce the following:

1. Increasing skill in performance facility, music reading and notation, composition, and conducting.

2. Growing awareness of the creative possibilities for relating music to other interests and experiences.

3. Expanding need for more information, skill, and experience. As the students grow more musically articulate (able to perform and create), it is the teacher's role to stimulate their need for further exploration. How did creative people (such as composers) in other eras solve tasks similar to those that the students have dealt with? What type of musical compositions existed that are related to the efforts the students are making? Are the students aware of how composers solved the problems of combining dramatic action with music (the study of opera, musical shows, ballet, Wagner, Rodgers and Hammerstein, Gilbert and Sullivan, Stravinsky, Tchaikovsky, etc.)? Can the students improve their creative work by examining the techniques other creators used? How does the use of varied rhythm (dynamics, timbre) change in various eras (jazz-rock, classical, romantic, impressionistic, contemporary)?

The activities in Phase II involve two basic ideas:

1. Continued efforts to improve skill (improvisation, notation, conducting, performance, etc.).

2. Intellectual and experiential inquiry into the full breadth of music style and technique. This inquiry might be divided into the following developmental areas:

    (a)   music and theater
    (b)   music and movement
    (c)   musical innovation
    (d)   music of the media
    (e)   music of tradition

LESSON PLAN FORM

CREATIVITY SOURCE

Class:

Date:

Phase	Strategy	Tactics	Materials (if any)	Alternative Tactics
II	1.	1.	1.	1.

Phase III: DEVELOPMENTAL INVOLVEMENT

Phase III is concerned with material at the point where many teachers often begin their work with students. This is understandable, since involvement in this area is related to the exploration and acquisition of musical facts. Listening to recorded performance of the musical repertoire, reading about composers, styles, periods, and musical techniques are the standard procedures utilized. In the Improvisational Method outlined in this book, these efforts, along with other significant activities, continue as major experiences in the development of musicianship. The main differences between the study of these areas is as follows:

1. The students become involved in the core of musical experience *as a result* of their attempts to make music on their own terms. Continuing involvement, along with guidance by the teacher, indicates to the student that he needs to know more (history, listening, reading, creating), and be able to perform more capably in order to increase his potential for personal success in creating through music. Thus listening to a Mozart opera is necessitated by the *student's* need (not just the teacher's need) to understand how speech patterns with musical accompaniment are handled by someone who has had success in doing this (Mozart). An analysis of this technique affords insight to the student, who may be seeking to apply them to the creation of a song, a "music drama" (a play with music), or even a staged musical show. Students who write poetry and wish to create a musical background, or a class presenting a play and wishing to intensify the dramatic quality through music, would do well to listen to the recorded performances of blues singers, folk singers, musical narratives (such as Copland's "A Lincoln Portrait"), Broadway show material (for example, "West Side Story"), leit-motif (a theme characterizing a specific character or situation) in

Wagnerian operas, in addition to Mozart, Verdi, and Rossini operas.

2. The major emphasis in Phase III is on creating, doing, experimenting, relating, and innovating (the student can consider any new personal experience as innovative). Students are urged in this phase to increasingly notate, "orchestrate," perform, improvise, and conduct. Thus intellectual investigation, accomplished through listening, reading, or analyzing, is a part of creating a musical product, but *doing* is the major focus. In the first stages, the musical product might be a notated composition or a primitive keyboard improvisation on the black notes. The teacher's role in this case is to direct the students to sources which will broaden their awareness, and then offer musical expertise in facilitating the students' creative efforts. A high level of personal musical activity leading to a wide range of musical products is the goal.

To summarize, the goal of Phase III is to afford each student opportunities to experience music through personal performance and activity. These activities will include: reading, analyzing, listening, composing, singing, conducting, orchestrating, writing, and improvising. Before proceeding to specific tactics that are related to the Creativity Sources of Phase III, a short description of each of the suggested developmental areas is given.

Developmental Areas

Music and theater: Inquiry in this area includes listening to recordings and reading about opera, as well as Broadway and off-Broadway productions. Investigation of musical works can range from the standard opera repertoire to such productions as "Jesus Christ, Superstar," Leonard Bernstein's "Mass," "Hair," "The King and I," "The Sound of Music," and the older productions, "Showboat," "Porgy and Bess," and "Oklahoma."

Music and movement: This area includes the ballet, social dances of various cultures and historical eras, and the ceremonial movements associated with or accompanied by music. Investigation may cover a wide variety of composers: Stravinsky—"The Firebird," "Petrouchka," "Rite of Spring"; Prokofiev—"Scythian Suite," "Romeo and Juliet," "Cinderella"; Shostakovitch—"Age of Gold"; Aaron Copland—"Appalachian Spring," "Billy the Kid," "Rodeo"; Leonard Bernstein—"Fancy Free," "Age of Anxiety," "Mass"; and so forth. Additionally, there are the popular dances of America (Charleston, Fox Trot, Jitterbug, Monkey, Twist, Bugaloo, Funky Chicken, etc.); Latin America (Tango, Mambo, Cha-Cha); Europe (Polka, Waltz, Hora, Irish Jig); and the Far East to be explored.

Musical innovation: This area covers a wide range of musical activity, including Aleatoric (John Cage, Henry Cowell, Karlheinz Stockhausen, etc.); Musique-Concrete (Edgar Varese, Carl Ruggles, etc.); Electronic (Pierre Boulez, Milton Babbitt); Improvisation (the entire scope of jazz activity and some aspects of rock, Lukas Foss, Gunther Schuller, John Lewis, etc.); Serial (Arnold Schoenberg, Alban Berg, Anton Webern, etc.).

Music of the media: Included in this area is the music used on television, motion pictures, radio, and light shows. The function and creation of music as related to backgrounds, themes, and commercials would come under investigation.

Music of tradition: This area encompasses the various periods, styles and forms of music, humanities-centered investigation, biographical inquiry, and exploration into the elements of traditional composition and performance practice. Some sample applications of Phase III activities related to each Creativity Source are indicated in the following pages.

Creativity Source-*Voice*

Strategy: To expand musical creativity and productivity while exploring all aspects of past and present musical accomplishment.

Tactics: In this sample case, the teacher has determined that student inquiry will be directed toward the developmental area, *music and tradition.* This is a personal choice, since another teacher might prefer to study in a different musical area.

(T) "Class, your individual groups produced some very interesting improvisations last time. Did you notice any difference in the way the improvisation sounded when you used the Alberti bass, compared to the rock basses? Do them again and see if you can find any."

(S) Individual groups perform. Students find that there does not seem to be a marked difference between the performance of Alberti bass improvisations and rock-type works.

(T) "By performing your improvisations of these two different basses in a similar way, you point up some interesting issues. First, is the function of a typical rock bass the same as an Alberti bass?"

(S) Students do not appear to know if there is any difference in function.

(T) "Okay, let's use our ears to test the question. First, I'm going to play a rock record. It's called   and is performed by   . I will follow that with a recording of the 'Piano Sonata in C Major, K.#545,' written by Wolfgang Amadeus Mozart. Let's listen." The teacher plays relatively short excerpts of each recording. "What differences did you hear in the bass parts?"

(S) "On the rock record, the bass is louder, more prominent . . . it's heavier . . . it seems to be as important as the melody, or even more important. On the Mozart recording, the Alberti bass is much quieter than the melody; the bass seems to have a different sound quality than the melody; the bass is only an accompaniment to the melody; the Mozart seems to have a different sound or color than the rock record."

(T) "You have made some very good points. The rock recording *is* different from the Mozart in sound quality (timbre) and balance and function between melody and accompaniment (harmony). Please listen to excerpts from these recordings again, *analyzing* the specific differences in the bass part. Write the differences down . . . then return to the small groups you were in and experiment through improvisations until you feel you have altered the timbre and balance of the bass and melody, so that they function according to the desired style (rock versus Alberti). Be sure to select a conductor to lead you in your improvisations."

(S) Students listen, analyze, and return to their groups. Some find that the sounds used in a rock performance need to be different from a Mozart (Classical period) setting. It appears that rock often uses guttural pointed sounds ("dop, da"), while the Classical period uses lighter, detached sounds (doot). Students experiment through vocal improvisations and then perform their improvisations.

(T) "Good, then there *is* a difference in the way the music of various periods sounds. Mozart was a composer in the Classical period (18th century). Are you able to produce the musical sound quality of different eras through your improvisation?"

(S) "What other eras are there? What does the music of other eras sound like? Who are some of the composers of different eras?"

(T) "You have asked some fascinating questions. Let's try to come up with some answers." The teacher plays excerpts from a variety of records, including Corelli, Scarlatti (harpsichord), Beethoven (5th Symphony or a piano sonata), Berlioz, Wagner, Debussy, Copland, Gershwin, Bartok, etc. Students analyze the excerpts for differences

(T) "Have you wondered why the music of different eras sounds different?

(S) "It probably has something to do with the style of life in different eras, maybe with what composers were trying to achieve."

(T) "Okay, let's investigate lives and styles in the different eras. If you like, we can divide the workload. As there are five small groups in the class, one group will explore the Baroque, another the Classical period, one of the Romantic period, another the Impressionistic, and the fifth the Contemporary period. After you have completed your research (a wide variety of research materials is available including library texts and several standard classroom history-listening series), create an example of that style through an improvisation that you will notate using musical or functional notation (depending on the musical maturity of the group). Be sure each one of you gets a chance to conduct his own improvisational score and that all have sufficient and good reasons for your musical decisions."

(S) Students read about composers, listen to music, analyze the varieties of techniques and elements, experiment in groups through improvisation, conducting, and notation, and finally reassemble as a class for the presentation of individual performances.

Extended activity may be further directed to show how the constituent elements of music (rhythm, melody, harmony, form) operate in various styles, varieties of performance techniques, and so forth. Teachers and students should also be encouraged to use whatever song materials are available.

Enrichment Activities

1. Draw different patterns of form on the blackboard (ABA, ABACA rondo, theme and variations, passacaglia, etc.). Ask the students to investigate these forms, listen to recordings, and sing musical examples, then motivate the group to create improvisations, using these design patterns.

2. Select a song that is representative of a particular period and sing it. Ask the class to improvise their own compositions based on the style and techniques of the song they have just sung.

Creativity Source-*Instruments*

Strategy: To expand musical creativity and productivity while exploring all aspects of past and present musical accomplishment.

Tactics: In this instance, the teacher has determined that student inquiry will be directed toward the developmental area, *music and movement.* Again, this choice is up to the individual teacher who has set specific goals for a class and who understands the needs of the students.

(T)　"Music serves many functions in our lives. Through the ages, man has moved to music in a variety of ways. From the jungles of Southeast Asia to the Scottish Highlands, music has served man's needs to express himself through movement, often in a way that is characteristic of his geographical or cultural environment. If, for instance, you were asked to create a tango, how would you begin?"

(S)　No answer.

(T)　"Okay, since you don't know what a tango sounds like, let's listen to a recording of 'Tango in D Major' by Isaac Albeniz."

(S)　Students listen to a short excerpt.

(T)　"As the record is played again, lightly tap the rhythmic motif (main rhythmic idea of the composition).''

(S)   Students listen, tap rhythm: $\frac{2}{4}$ ♩. ♪ ♪ ♪ ♪

(T)   "Let's clap it several times (pause). Now, I am going to clap the motif to you as you write it down."

(S)   Students have considerable trouble, which requires the teacher's help (have students first write down even eight notes, then fit dotted quarter and eighth notes in between). Corrections are made until everyone has written the motif properly.

(T)   "Everyone clap the motif; keep repeating it, achieving some of the flavor of South America, where the tango came from." $\frac{2}{4}$ ♩. ♪ ♪ ♪ ♪

(S)   Students experiment first with clapping. At the teacher's suggestion, the students move to instruments, possibly nonpitched or environmental at first.

(T)   "Let's use the tango pattern as the motif along with other rhythms and play them with varied dynamics. I would like you to break up into improvisation groups and, as a group, write a story. Then you have several choices:

    (a)   Improvise an instrumental composition based on the tango motif and your corresponding story, which will be danced by one or more members of your group.

    (b)   Create a story and musical accompaniment which includes class participation involving some type of group dance experience.

    (c)   Create an improvised composition which could serve as an appropriate dance accompaniment or an enjoyable listening experience."

(S)   Students perform various choices (receptivity to the concepts of dance will, in most cases, be related to the grade or age level of the students). Students discuss compositions, stories, or dance movements.

(T)   "Rock music of the 1950s and 60s produced some unusual dances."

(S)   Yeah, the Frug . . . Watusi . . . Monkey . . . Twist . . . Chicken . . . Bugaloo . . ."

(T)   "Okay, we are going to listen to examples of some of these. You will listen for the rhythmic motif in the piece, usually in the bass voice. Don't worry, I'll help you with it. I'll play each recording enough times so that you will be able to write the rhythm. (Recordings with highly repetitive and visible patterns should be used.) When you have gotten it, I want you to return to your groups, where you will take the motif and create a composition that falls into the area of choices I gave you before. This time, be sure that you create a melody that is clearly defined and singable."

(S)   Students listen, take rhythmic motifs for dictation, return to their groups, and improvise compositions related to the three choices discussed earlier. (If the students are completely unable to identify a motif, then the teacher will create one and clap or play it on the piano.)

(T)   The teacher leads the class in an open discussion evaluating the dances. This discussion is led in such a way that questions arise as to how various composers write for the dance. "In this example, class, Leonard Bernstein, in 'The Rumble' from 'West Side Story,' sought to depict a gang fight occurring on a street in New York City. Listen to it and analyze the types of movements suggested by the music."

(S)   "Sounds like guys are jumping at each other, like they are wrestling each other to the ground; sounds like a knife fight."

(T)   "Now, listen to it again, this time noting *what* the composer did to convey the mental picture you received."

(S)   Students listen and analyze techniques that are used.

(T)   "Return to your groups with your instruments. Create the same feeling that Bernstein created by improvising with the techniques that you explored previously."

(S)   Students experiment, then perform for the class. Later, each group will tape their compositions for analysis and discussion. It is becoming increasingly obvious that students need more skill on their instruments in order to perform. The teacher will begin to introduce various activities intended to strengthen the student's facility for performing and controlling his instrument. In the elementary grades, students playing melody instruments might use the *Creating Music* * series, while in the upper grades (junior and senior high school) the *Basic Training Course for Beginning Bands* * or the *Learn to Play* * series for all instruments may be used. Class activity is now divided between further listening experiences, increased analysis and discussion of musical techniques, and the acquisition of instrumental skills on varied-pitch and nonpitched instruments.

Musical success is often measured by students and teachers in terms of performance ability. Increasing emphasis on performance achievement and the translation of these skills into personal creative expression (through improvisation and composition) will be better accomplished if a regular place is found for both of these points in the class program. Thus each time a class meets, some activity involving development of skill and their creative application should be included.

Enrichment Activities

1. Select a recording that demonstrates how various composers created dance-like compositions reflecting the special style and character of their country. Examples: Chopin—Mazurkas and Waltzes; Liszt—Hungarian dances; Smetana—"The Moldau" (the section called "Peasant Wedding"); Debussy—"Golliwogs Cakewalk" (ragtime dance rhythm); Copland—"El Salon Mexico," "The Dance Symphony," "Rodeo" (the four dance episodes, "Corrale Nocturne," "Buckaroo Holiday," "Saturday Night Waltz," and Hoedown"); Tchaikovsky—"The Nutcracker Suite," 3rd movement of "Violin Concerto in D." Analyze, discuss, and re-create in instrumental improvisational experiences by isolating rhythms and then developing them through performance.

2. Select any article on the front page of the morning newspaper. Each group might select a different one and then create an instrumental improvisation/composition, including narrative (acting out) and dancing that captures the spirit or message of the article.

3. Students select an object that implies movement—a train, plane, balloon floating in the air, a bird, boat, a bottle floating in the water. They create the score for an improvisation/composition depicting that object, then perform it.

Creativity Source-*Keyboard*

Strategy: To expand musical creativity and productivity while exploring all aspects of past and present musical accomplishment.

Tactics: In this instance, the teacher has determined that student inquiry will be directed toward the developmental area, *music and innovation.*

(T) "Up to now, we have been using musical materials that probably sound quite conventional to you. The scales and modes you have experimented with at the keyboard have been around for a long time. There was a point in the history of music when a new scale, even a major scale, seemed like quite an innovation. Some of you might be interested to know that our major scale was used by the ancient Greeks. However, it sounded quite different because the Greeks used a different system of tuning. In fact, it wasn't until 1750 that equal temperament (a system of tuning that makes all tones of the same pitch alike on an instrument) was clearly established as the standard." Appropriate at this point would be listening to and discussing J.S. Bach's "Well-Tempered Clavier," with a performance of the selections chosen from harpsichord (Landowska), piano (Tureck), and synthesizer ("Switched on Bach"/Columbia MS—7194).

(S) Students listen to these recordings, with the discussion developing around differences in sound between the same compositions.

(T) "The composer has continually sought to develop new and challenging directions in which to express himself. I will play two different recordings for you, each an example of a radical departure by its composer. Listen to both of them and write down the ways in which you think these works represent a new direction."

The teacher then plays a short excerpt from any 12-tone piece.

Suggested recordings are:

Arnold Schoenberg	Piano Concerto, Opus 42
	Variations for Orchestra, Opus 31
	The Wind Quintet, Opus 25
	The Third String Quartet, Opus 30
Anton Webern	Cantata No. 1, Opus 29
Alban Berg	Lulu or Wozzeck

Next, the teacher plays short excerpts from either example of Musique-Concrete, Chance music, Improvisation, or Electronic. Suggested recordings in this area include:

Musique-Concrete

Edgar Varese	Deserts
	Density 21.5
	Ionisation
	Integrates
George Antheil	Ballet Mecanique
Carl Ruggles	Portals
	Evocation

Chance music (Aleatoric)

John Cage	Concerto for Prepared Piano
	The Seasons
	Third Construction
Henry Cowell	Mosaic
	26 Simultaneous Mosaics
Karlheinz Stockhausen	Momente Carre
	Klavierstucke XI
	Zyklus

Improvisation

Jazz and rock recordings

Gunther Schuller	Conversations
John Lewis	Sketch for Double Quartet
Lukas Foss	Time Cycle

Electronic

Otto Leuning	Fantasy in Space Low Speed
Vladamir Ussachevsky	Rhapsodic Variations for Tape Recorder and Orchestra A Poem in Cycles and Bells
Pierre Boulez	Structures
Milton Babbitt	Ensembles for Synthesizer
Karlheinz Stockhausen	Electronic Studies

After the playing of these recording examples, the discussion focuses on the "strange sounds" of the recordings.

(S) "That's not music, it's noise . . . boy, that's terrible . . . it's great . . . Some of the electronic records sound like rock sounds . . . . anyone could do that."

(T) "In each case, the music you heard, whether or not you found it appealing, represents the development of a new idea. The Schoenberg composition, for example, is based on a controlled way of creating music by using 12 tones. In the way that Schoenberg developed the 12-tone system, the 12 notes are placed in an arbitrary arrangement (called a 12-tone row) and are not allowed to appear again in that sequence until all the 12 tones have been used. The tones may be used individually, in small groups of tones, or in chords, but still in the order of the original row. Let's create a 12-tone row."

(S) Students arbitrarily call out 12 tones which the teacher writes on the board and each student writes in his manuscript book.

(T) "Okay, first line of students come up with your manuscript books and play the original row."

(S) About 10 or 12 students are heard, with each student individually playing his row.

(T) "Obviously, a 12-tone composer like Schoenberg would be terribly limited if that was all he had to work with. What are some other ways a composer might extend the use of the row?"

(S)   "Play it backwards."

(T)   "Excellent! That's just what they do. When an original row is written backwards, from right to left, it is called a *retrograde*. Write the retrograde of our row."

(S)   Students write the retrograde in their manuscript books.

(T)   "Next group, come up to the piano and let's have each one play the original row (O) and the retrograde (R)."

With the teacher's help, the students discover that the row can also be written turned upside down, *inverted* (I), and upside down and backwards, retrograde inversion (RI). The teacher may call several students to the piano at one time, having each student accomplish a different task. For example, one might be asked to play the O (original) and I (inversion), another the O and RI (retrograde inversion), and so on. Students should be encouraged to vary dynamics, rhythms, registers, and groupings of notes. This constitutes improvisational experience. Later, students will be asked to sketch a score that will utilize many arrangements of the row. Students in the lower grades who have limited facility might reduce a row to six notes. Later, students might meet in small groups, create a row with all its ramifications, and then individually perform it. Clear evidence of improvisational activity will be observed in the varieties of rhythms, registers, dynamics, and type of row variations that develop. It is suggested that students tape record their 12-tone "compositions" so that the class may have sufficient time to hear, analyze, and discuss them.

The activity developed in relation to the 12-tone technique may be extended over a period of time to Musique-Concrete, Chance music, Improvisation, and Electronic. Here are some suggestions for application:

Musique-Concrete is a type of music that is created when "natural" sound and sound effects are recorded on tape whose speed is then altered. Students might improvise melodies at the piano, record them, and play them back at various speeds. Then they should design a broader improvisation, using varied piano "effects" created by holding down the pedal, lightly running their fingers across the strings, and the combining of these techniques with other sounds (whistling, the voice, instruments, the opening and closing of a door, etc.). Students should be thoroughly instructed in the proper use and care of the piano in these experimental encounters. Creative exploration should never allow abuse of musical instruments. These improvisations might easily be individual or group projects. Improvisations will be recorded in the manner already prescribed for Musique-Concrete.

Chance music is a compositional process through which the composer relies on random chance to determine the construction and development of his composition. Students might write several notes or improvisational instructions for performance on several different pages, and randomly shuffle them from time to time during a performance. Or a group of notes may be written out, with the student-pianist improviser playing a particular note when a specific sound is made. A group, in this case, may design a chance piece in which a *C* is played when someone in the group whistles, a *D* for a clap, an *E* for a foot stamp, and so forth. The group would be randomly improvising their sounds. Students, in most cases, will have many creative ideas for this type of activity.

Improvisation refers to both variation and spontaneous creation in relation to a specific idea. Thus students with minimal piano ability might be asked to write a short melody and then vary it at the piano by playing it differently each time, either by changing the rhythm, dynamics, tempo, or accents. More mature students might be aided in developing insight into chords (even simple I IV V chords), and improvise on them by playing the chord tones of each chord in varying order and rhythm.

Electronic music is created by using an electrical piece of equipment. A careful investigation of *The New World of Electronic Music* * by Walter Sear will give teachers much insight into a contemporary musical area in which many students display a considerable interest.

Involvement in these activities will be most significant to each individual student as the teacher aids the student in transferring the insights gained in a specific innovating area to a credible piano improvisational experience.

Enrichment Activities

1. Create a "jam session." Encourage individuals or small groups to write a melody with empty bars for the performer to improvise his own material. After each student or group has performed, have students exchange material, which will then be performed at the piano. Later, other instruments and voice parts, improvised, notated, or partially notated to allow for improvisation, can be generated.

2. Through research (reading) and listening, explore other innovating musicians in addition to those mentioned in this text (Beethoven, Berlioz, Debussy, Bach).

3. Create an improvisation/composition which involves using the piano in a way you have never used it in performance before.

LESSON PLAN FORM

CREATIVITY SOURCE

Class:

Date:

Phase	Strategy	Tactics	Materials (if any)	Alternative Tactics
III	1.	1.	1.	1.

ZODIAC
A VOCAL IMPROVISATION ENCOUNTER

SUGGESTIONS FOR PERFORMANCE

Zodiac is designed to afford singers the *joy of performing* along with the *excitement of creating*. The following suggestions will aid in attaining these goals.

B Divide the chorus equally into 1st chorus and 2nd chorus, each singing the indicated part.

B1 Select 12 small groups, each representing a different Zodiac sign. The groups might be composed of singers actually born under that sign, by voice part, by location in the chorus or by any means deemed appropriate by the conductor and/or chorus members. The entire chorus sings the first 2 bars ("All") which is answered by the indicated Zodiac group.

C Add 2-4 tambourines playing lightly.

D Improvisational Encounter Section

   1 - Piano plays repeated bass pattern as indicated group speaks its name to the notated rhythm.

   2 - One individual from the group slowly and clearly speaks the characteristics of the Zodiac sign as indicated in the top of each box. (Piano continues without interruption.)

   3 - Group improvises on tactic a, b, c or any other deemed suitable. Be adventurous!

   4 - Upon completing improvisation, pianist proceeds to next Zodiac group pattern (1/2 step higher) without interruption. The succeeding groups perform using the same performance techniques.

E Add many tambourines.

F Select small group to continuously chant "ooh" sound.

Dedicated to Lillian Messicks and the Lloyd Harbor School Chorus

ZODIAC

A VOCAL IMPROVISATION ENCOUNTER *
(Two Part Chorus with Piano Accompaniment)

BERT KONOWITZ
and
ORLANDO DI GIROLAMO

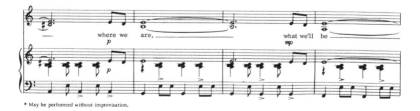

* May be performed without improvisation.

© Copyright MCMLXXI by Alfred Music Co., Inc.
International Copyright Secured   Made in U. S. A.   All Rights Reserved

those dis - tant stars.

what do they

say?

1st Chorus **B**

The 12 signs of the Zo - di - ac.

2nd Chorus

12 signs of the Zo - di - ac.

B¹ All

Aries Group - 1st time
Taurus Group - 2nd time

First sign of the — Zo - di - ac, Ar - ies, the ram.
Sec - ond sign of the Zo - di - ac, Tau - rus, the bull.

67

Tenth sign of the Zo - di - ac, Cap - ri - corn, the goat,

All *Capricorn Group*

Elev - enth sign of the Zo - di - ac, A - qua - ri - us, the wa - ter boy.

All *Aquarius Group*

Twelfth sign of the Zo - di - ac, Pis - ces, the fish.

All *Pisces Group*

C

Tambourine

Tamb. cont.

p

* if you wish to perform Zodiac without the improvisation encounter, at this point skip to D.

Signs of the Zo - di - ac reach a - cross the

sky call - ing out to tell ____ us,

tell us, _____ tell us what, _____

Tamb. out

_ tell us all _____ that you are.

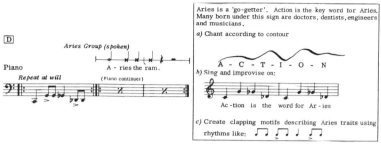

Aries is a 'go-getter'. Action is the key word for Aries. Many born under this sign are doctors, dentists, engineers and musicians.

a) Chant according to contour

A - C - T - I - O - N

b) Sing and improvise on:

Ac -tion is the word for Ar - ies

c) Create clapping motifs describing Aries traits using rhythms like:

(left staff: D — Aries Group (spoken) — Piano — A - ries the ram. — Repeat at will — (Piano continues))

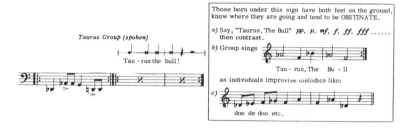

Those born under this sign have both feet on the ground, know where they are going and tend to be OBSTINATE.

a) Say, "Taurus, The Bull" *pp, p, mf, f, ff, fff* ...... then contrast.

b) Group sings

Tau - rus, The Bu - ll

as individuals improvise melodies like:

c)

doo de doo etc.

(left staff: Taurus Group (spoken) — Tau -rus the bull!)

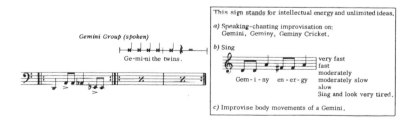

This sign stands for intellectual energy and unlimited ideas.

a) Speaking-chanting improvisation on: Gemini, Geminy, Geminy Cricket.

b) Sing

Gem - i - ny en - er - gy

very fast
fast
moderately
moderately slow
slow
Sing and look very tired.

c) Improvise body movements of a Gemini.

(left staff: Gemini Group (spoken) — Ge-mi-ni the twins.)

Cancer Group (spoken)

Can - cer the crab.

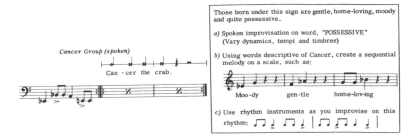

Those born under this sign are gentle, home-loving, moody and quite possessive.

a) Spoken improvisation on word, "POSSESSIVE" (Vary dynamics, tempi and timbres)

b) Using words descriptive of Cancer, create a sequential melody on a scale, such as:

Moo-dy   gen-tle   home-lov-ing

c) Use rhythm instruments as you improvise on this rhythm:

Leo Group (spoken)

Le - o the Li - on

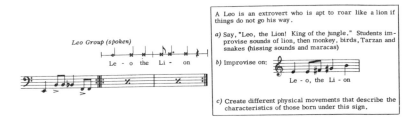

A Leo is an extrovert who is apt to roar like a lion if things do not go his way.

a) Say, "Leo, the Lion! King of the jungle." Students improvise sounds of lion, then monkey, birds, Tarzan and snakes (hissing sounds and maracas)

b) Improvise on:

Le - o, the Li - on

c) Create different physical movements that describe the characteristics of those born under this sign.

Virgo Group (spoken)

Vir - go the Vir - gin

Virgo is the most humorous sign of the Zodiac. She's courteous, friendly, kind, and so very funny.

a) Ha! Ha! Ha! (Improvise with laughing sounds)

b) Clap or play

c) Sing an improvisation on:

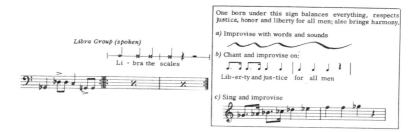

Libra Group (spoken)

Li - bra the scales

One born under this sign balances everything, respects justice, honor and liberty for all men; also brings harmony.

a) Improvise with words and sounds

b) Chant and improvise on:

Lib-er-ty and jus-tice for all men

c) Sing and improvise

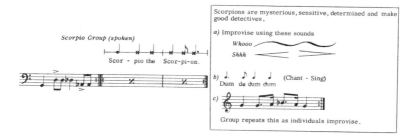

Scorpio Group (spoken)

Scor - pio the Scor-pi-on.

Scorpions are mysterious, sensitive, determined and make good detectives.

a) Improvise using these sounds

Whooo

Shhh

b) Dum de dum dum (Chant - Sing)

c)

Group repeats this as individuals improvise.

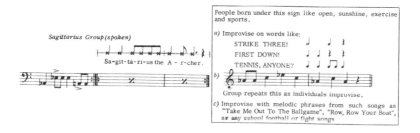

Sagittarius Group (spoken)

Sa-git-ta-ri-us the A - r-cher.

People born under this sign like open, sunshine, exercise and sports.

a) Improvise on words like:

STRIKE THREE!

FIRST DOWN!

TENNIS, ANYONE?

b)

Group repeats this as individuals improvise.

c) Improvise with melodic phrases from such songs as "Take Me Out To The Ballgame", "Row, Row Your Boat", or any school football or fight songs

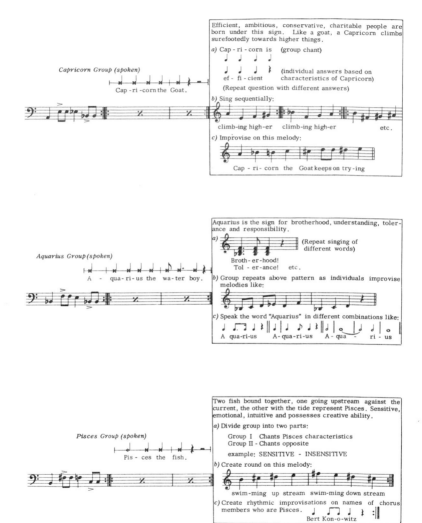

Efficient, ambitious, conservative, charitable people are born under this sign. Like a goat, a Capricorn climbs surefootedly towards higher things.

a) Cap - ri - corn is   (group chant)

ef - fi - cient   (individual answers based on characteristics of Capricorn)

(Repeat question with different answers)

b) Sing sequentially:

climb-ing high-er   climb-ing high-er   etc.

c) Improvise on this melody:

Cap - ri - corn the   Goat keeps on try-ing

Capricorn Group (spoken)

Cap-ri-corn the Goat.

Aquarius is the sign for brotherhood, understanding, toler-ance and responsibility.

a)   (Repeat singing of different words)

Broth-er-hood!
Tol - er-ance!   etc.

b) Group repeats above pattern as individuals improvise melodies like:

c) Speak the word "Aquarius" in different combinations like:

A qua-ri-us   A- qua-ri-us   A- qua - ri - us

Aquarius Group (spoken)

A - qua - ri - us the wa-ter boy.

Two fish bound together, one going upstream against the current, the other with the tide represent Pisces. Sensitive, emotional, intuitive and possesses creative ability.

a) Divide group into two parts:

Group I Chants Pisces characteristics
Group II - Chants opposite

example: SENSITIVE - INSENSITIVE

b) Create round on this melody:

swim-ming up stream swim-ming down stream

c) Create rhythmic improvisations on names of chorus members who are Pisces.

Bert Kon-o-witz

Pisces Group (spoken)

Pis - ces the fish.

Upon completion of improvisation, proceed to letter E without interruption.

74

Smaller Group

Ooh _____

Signs of the Zo - di - ac reach a - cross the sky

Ooh _____

call - ing out to tell ___ us, who we are, _____

rallentando *spoken* *rit.*

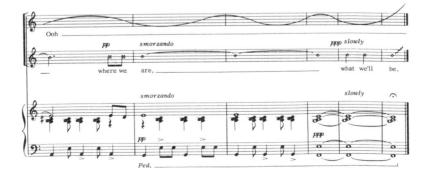

Ooh _____

where we are, _____ what we'll be.

smorzando *slowly*

Ped. _____

76

APPENDIX B

Song Performance in The Improvisational Method

The Improvisational Method may be used to expand on the traditional aspects of the singing experience. In utilizing improvisation in this manner, the student has the opportunity to combine traditional singing experiences with creative musical activity. Thus, both students and teachers have an opportunity to deal with familiar musical experiences while developing skill and insights into creative and self-expressive activities.

The techniques indicated in the example given below may be transferred to *any* song, whatever the character, style, or grade level.

Song: "Red River Valley"

Form: The overall design of the performance of "Red River Valley" will be in three parts.

   1st part: Students sing "Red River Valley" as written, followed by a transition leading to the 2nd part.

   2nd part: Improvisational section

   3rd part: Return to singing "Red River Valley"

Optional Coda

Teaching Tactics:

Step No. 1 —Sing "Red River Valley" as written

Red River Valley

Refrain:

From this val - ley they say you are go - ing, ____ We will
Come and sit by my side if you love me, ____ Do not

miss your bright eyes and your smile,__ For they say you are tak - ing the
has - ten to bid me a - dieu,__ But re - mem - ber the Red Riv - er

sun - shine,__ That bright - en'd our path - way a while.____
val - ley, ____ And the girl who has loved you so true.____

Step No. 2—Develop a transition from "Red River Valley" to the improvisation. Here are some suggestions for creating a transition:

After the last tone of the song is sung ("G"), proceed directly ahead without pause by singing a drone bass. The drone bass might be any of the following:

a. A stationary, repetitive "G" sung as whole notes.

b. A stationary, repetitive "G" sung in more varied rhythms. The rhythms are dictated by the teacher to the students by bending the left arm at the elbow so that the finger tips are pointing upward, and tapping the desired rhythms with the right hand on the underside of the left forearm (now facing the students). These rhythms might include the following:

c. A melodic repetitive motif.

After the transition has been effected, the students are ready to move on to the Improvisation section (2nd part).

Step No. 3—The Improvisation section will include some element of "Red River Valley." The improvisational materials and techniques might include any of the following suggestions:

a. Improvising on the chord structure of "Red River Valley"— As the students sing the chord structure of "Red River Valley" I/I/IV/IV/I/I/V/V/I/I/IV/IV/I/I/V/I/I/, create varied accompaniment patterns with block, alberti or oom-pah basses. As the entire group continues to sing this chord progression, invite various individuals and/or small groups of students to sing chord tone or scale improvisations.

OR

have the students sing a new chord progression which is dictated by the conductor (teacher or student) with hand signals.

OR

have students sing an accompaniment using only a I chord as other students improvise chord tone and scale improvisations of that chord.

b. Improvising on the spirit or character of "Red River Valley"—

Choose specific words or phrases found in the song. These selections might include, "you are going," "your bright eyes," "the sunshine," etc. As the majority of the students softly sing the chordal background, the individual student will chant, speak, or sing his phrase aloud, using a variety of techniques, including changes of pitch, dynamics, accents, timbre, rhythm, and order of words. The teacher may aid the improvisor by suggesting variations through hand signals. Be sure to give many students a chance for solo improvisation. Finally, all the students might improvise their own materials at the same time.

OR

develop "sound collages" related to the spirit, geographic setting, or mood of the song. "Sound collages" are improvised compositions consisting of a variety of vocal sounds that describe a specific idea or situation. As the chordal accompaniment is continued by most of students, have individuals or small groups improvise sounds which might include:

sounds of the "West"; various animals found on the prairie, the Western desert at daybreak, at noon when it is 123 degrees, at sunset, during the long, dark night.

Additional sound collages might be developed from students drawings, from slides that were taken on a trip, from posters, pictures in books and magazines, etc.

c. Improvising a dramatization based on the contents or spirit of "Red River Valley"—

Develop a dramatization related to the contents of the song. Thus, as the group sings the chordal background, small groups are selected to improvise a dramatization related to some aspect of "Red River Valley." During the "dramas" it is best to have the background hummed. Stage props and characteristic clothing will provide charm to this activity.

Step No. 4—Just before the completion of the improvisational section, point to the top of your head, which is the signal for Da Capo (return to the beginning of the song). Then give a downbeat, which will be a signal for the entire group to return to singing the original version of "Red River Valley." Sing the song through as written. As an added attraction, you might have students improvise a short coda by having the larger number of students sing the song while some of the previous improvisations are repeated in miniature. You might also have the students fade out gradually, while individually improvising a word, phrase, or sound of their own choice.

ANNOTATED BIBLIOGRAPHY

CREATIVITY SOURCE—VOICE

Konowitz, Bert. *Cantus Firmus* (SSA). New York: Alfred Publishing Co., Inc., 1969.

> While this composition might prove to be difficult for the young performer, there are many techniques such as choral speaking, scat singing (jazz and rock), and chanting that may serve as a model for developing relevant materials at various grade levels.

_____. *Growing Up Free!* (Unison-2 part). New York: Alfred Publishing Co., Inc., 1973.

> This composition can be performed by students at all levels. There is ample opportunity for vocal, dance, and dramatic improvisation, which also invites the audience to participate. Contains optional guitar, bass, and drums accompaniment.

_____. *The Last Word* (SATB). New York: Alfred Publishing Co., Inc., 1972.

> For experienced vocal groups, but also can be utilized as a model for initiating improvisational experiences that invite the student to use his spontaneous emotional reactions to various stimuli. Audience participation is encouraged.

_____. *Zodiac* (Unison-2 part). New York: Alfred Publishing Co., Inc., 1971.

> The rock-flavored melody gives way to an extended improvisational section which enourages the choir to divide into 12 groups, with each one improvising on a different Zodiac sign.

_____. *The Bert Konowitz Vocal Improvisation Method.* New York: Alfred Publishing Co., Inc., 1971.

> A complete course of study that develops vocal improvisation skills in both jazz and rock styles. A glossary of vocal improvisation hand signals for the teacher, as well as creative projects for students, is included.

Palmer, Willard A. *Choral Improvisations on the Poem Ozymandias.* New York: Alfred Publishing Co., Inc., 1970.

> A creative opportunity for students to explore a range of improvisational techniques through choral speaking and singing.

McElheran, Brock. *A Bilogy* (4-part chorus, a capella). New York: Carl Fisher, Inc.

A challenging work for students in the upper grades. This composition serves as an example of the innovative techniques found in contemporary choral notation.

_____. *Here Comes the Avant-Garde* New York: Oxford University Press.

_____. *Patterns in Sound: Sections A, B and C* (SSAATBB unaccompanied). New York: Oxford University Press.

Innovative conducting, improvisation, and notation experiences make this a demanding musical encounter.

CREATIVITY SOURCE—KEYBOARD

Adams, Paul. *Folk Rock for the Student Pianist* (piano and guitar). New York: Mills Music Co.

An elementary level text for both the teacher and student to develop fundamental rock skills.

Bergerac, Nicole. *Sassafras and Marmalade.* New York: Schroeder and Gunther, Inc.

Pages 6 and 7 contain a keyboard improvisational experience geared to the young player.

Covello, Stephen. *The Little Avant-Garde* (A Piano Method for the Pre-Schooler). New York: Schroeder and Gunther, Inc.

A truly innovative approach to teaching music to very young players, stressing improvisation and contemporary notation. Can be used at any level of instruction that has not had introductory work with twentieth-century performance and notation.

Konowitz, Bert. *The Complete Rock Piano Method* (with accompanying record for add-a-part performances). New York: Alfred Publishing Co., Inc.

Serves as a guide to developing rock musicianship through improvisation, technique, solo performance, and duet performance. The accompanying record offers students an opportunity to play along with a rhythm accompaniment composed of guitar, bass, and drums. .

_____. *Jazz for Piano.* Vols. 1 and 2. New York: Lee Roberts Music.

A sequentially structured approach to teaching jazz improvisation for the beginning improvisor. Attention is given to the techniques of rhythmic, melodic, and harmonic skills of jazz improvisation.

_____. *Jazz for Piano Recital Series* New York: Lee Roberts Music.

Blue Note Boogie
Choo, Choo Stomp
Jazz Spooks
Jazz Waltz
Lazy Daze
Poundin' the Beat
Raga Rock
Surf Swing
Time Changes

This is an individually published collection of short pieces that offer many opportunities for improvisation.

Pace, Robert. *Music for Piano, and Skills and Drills* (Books 1-6). New York: Lee Roberts Music

A carefully structured approach to teaching comprehensive musicianship and improvisation from the very beginning.

Palmer, Willard A. and Amanda Vick Lethco. *Creating Music at the Piano* New York: Alfred Publishing Co., Inc.

This is an attractive and imaginative approach to teaching a broad range of musical skills from the very beginning. Emphasis is continually placed on creative expansion of the given materials.

CREATIVITY SOURCE—INSTRUMENTS

Dennis, Brian. *Tetrahedron* (Instrumentation ad. lib with optional organ).

_____. *Aquarelle* (for solo piano and 6 percussion players).

Rands, Bernard. *Sound Patterns I* (for voices and hands).

Self, George. *Warwick* (for percussion, descant recorders, and piano).

Small, Christopher. *Black Cat* (for voices and percussion).

These compositions are published by Theodore Presser Co., Bryn Mawr, Pennsylvania. The imaginative and creatively challenging experiences are primarily for young players, although they can be used effectively with any level.

Allen, Stacey and Saul Feldstein. *Creating Music with Melody Instruments*
New York, Alfred Publishing Co., Inc.

A thoughtfully designed text that affords the very earliest players to gain
insights into musical concepts while learning to play. The recorder,
tonette, flutophone, or song flute can be used in a broad range of musical
experiences which include duet parts, rhythm parts, chord symbols for
autoharp and guitar and words for singing. This can be used effectively in
Phases II and III of the Improvisational Method.

_____. *Creating Music with Melody and Rhythm Instruments.* New York,
Alfred Publishing Co., Inc.

_____. *Creating Music with Guitar,* New York, Alfred Publishing Co.,
Inc.

All three of the Creating Music series may be correlated with the other
texts.

SUGGESTED READING

Cage, John, ed. *Notations.* New York, Something Else Press, 1967.
A brilliant presentation of innovative notational systems used by
twentieth-century composers.

Cope, David. *New Directions in Music.* Dubuque, Iowa: W.C. Brown Co.,
1971.
This small volume contains an abundance of information on evolving
techniques of musical creation found in twentieth-century music. An
especially useful chapter on improvisation is included.

Dwyer, Terrence. *Composing with Tape Recorders.* London: Oxford
University Press, 1971.
A primer that will aid teacher and student in developing skills for
creating musique-concrete. It is also very useful as a self-programmed
teaching text. Phase II and III activities will be benefited by the
techniques suggested in this book.

Fellerer, K.G., ed. *Anthology of Music: Improvisation in Nine Centuries of
Western Music.* Cologne, Germany: Arno Volk Verlag, 1961.
An authoritative and scholarly presentation of the development of
improvisation in the Western world. In addition to the historical
information, the creative teacher will find the information gleaned from
this text useful in developing creative approaches with traditional musical
experiences.

Kostelanetz, Richard. *John Cage.* New York: Praeger Publications Inc., 1970
Any teacher seeking to expand creative directions should become intensely aware of this, one of the most original thinkers of this century. The text offers many insights into the creative mind.

Paynter, John and Peter Aston. *Sound and Silence.* London: Cambridge University Press, 1970
Contains many classroom projects that afford students opportunities for creative exploration. Many of the projects included here will be useful in expanding on Phase I, II, and III activities.

Sear, Walter. *The New World of Electronic Music.* New York, Alfred Publishing Co., Inc., 1972.
Affords teacher and student a better understanding of electronic music and the synthesizer, while explaining the fundamentals of sound, electricity, music, and recording as a background for a practical description of electronic music, of synthesizers and their characteristics, and of the equipment itself. The information gained from this book can effectively be applied to Phase II and III experiences.

Source: Music of the Avant-Garde, 330 University Ave., Davis, California, Composer/Performer Edition.
A marvelous magazine. A must for the improvisational teacher.

INDEX

accents, 12

Alberti bass: *see* bass, Alberti

Aleatoric: *see* chance music

articulation, 26

augmentation, 25

bass: Alberti, 27, 31, 38, 48-49; broken chord, 27, 28, 31; drone, 17; Indian, 17; jazz, 27, 29; jazz-walking, 42; oom-pah, 27–28, 38; rock, 27, 29, 42, 48-49; single note, 31; waltz, 27, 38, 40; "Western," 17; *see also* chords; modes

Bernstein, Leonard, 47, 53

body: *see* instrument

chance (Aleatoric) music: John Cage, 47, 57; Henry Cowell, 47, 57; Karlheinz Stockhausen, 47, 57; suggested applications of, 60; suggested recordings of, 57

chords, 27-31, 39; in improvisation, 60; in 12-tone system, 58

chord tones, 29-30, 60

conducting: by students, 7-8, 25-26, 30, 33, 49-50; suggestions for, 5

Copland, Aaron, 45, 47, 55

Creativity Sources, 3–4, 22; phases of, 3; types of, 3

dance, 47, 55; Isaac Albeniz, "Tango in D Major," 51; Leonard Bernstein, "Age of Anxiety," 47, "Fancy Free," 47, "Mass," 47, "West Side Story," 53; Chopin, mazurkas and waltzes, 55; Aaron Copland, "Appalachian Spring," 47, "Billy the Kid," 47, "The Dance Symphony," 55, "Rodeo," 47, 55, "El Salon Mexico," 55; Debussy, "Golliwogs Cakewalk," 55; Liszt, "Hungarian Dances," 55; Prokofiev, "Cinderella," 47, "Romeo and Juliet," 47, "Scythian Suite," 47; rock music and, 52-53; Shostakovitch, "Age of Gold," 47; Smetana, "The Moldau," 55; Stravinsky, "The Firebird," 47, "Petrouchka," 47, "Rite of Spring," 47; tango motif, 51-52; Tchaikovsky, "The Nutcracker Suite," 55, "Violin Concerto in D," 55

dynamics, 6-7, 12, 18-19, 21; in dance, 52

electronic music: Milton Babbitt, 47, 58; Pierre Boulez, 47, 58; creation of, 34, 60; suggested recordings, 58

equal temperament (tuning), 56

equipment for classroom, 4

forms, ABA, 26, 50; ABACA rondo, 51; passacaglia, 51; rhapsody, 26; rondo, 26; theme and variations, 51

forte, 5

harmonic intervals, 37-38

harmonic pattern, 37-38, 39

harmony, 49

improvisation (style): creation of, 13, 60; Lukas Foss, 47, 57; John Lewis, 47, 57; Gunther Schuller, 47, 57; suggested recordings, 57

Improvisational Method, 1-2, 45

instrument, human body as, 10

instruments: categories of, 10-11; definition of, 10; electronic media as, 10, 34, 60; environmental, 10-11, 14, 32-34, 52; manufactured (orchestral), 11, 14

inversion (12-tone system), 59

jazz, 47, 57; see also bass

legato, 5, 26

leitmotif, 45-46

lesson plan form, 4, 24, 44, 62

melodies, 29-30, 48

modes: Dorian, 38, 40; Hindu (ragas), 42; Mixolydian, 38, 40

motif, 25

musical innovation, 47, 56-61; see also chance music; electronic music; improvisation; musique-concrete; serial music

musical periods (eras): chord patterns in, 31; differences among, 48-50

music and movement: see dance

music and theater, suggested recordings of, 47

music and tradition: see musical periods

music of the media, 21, 47

musique-concrete: Carl Ruggles, 47, 57; suggested applications of, 59-60; suggested recordings of, 57; Edgar Varese, 47, 57

notation systems: functional, 33, 37, 41, 50; standard (musical), 41, 50

oom-pah: see bass, oom-pah

operational plans, 3-4

phrasing, 20, 26

piano (musical direction), 5

pitch, 6, 26, 32

polyphony, 26

portamento, 26

punctuation, 26

questions and answers: contrasting, 12, 19; parallel, 11-12, 18-19

ragas: see modes, Hindu

recordings illustrative of: emotional themes, 26; Alberti bass, 48; dance, 47, 53; dance (tango), 51-52; innovation, 56-58; music in theater, 47

retrograde (12-tone system), 59

retrograde inversion, 59

retrograde motion, 25

rhythmic motif, 51-52

rhythmic ostinato, 8

rock bass: *see* bass, rock

scales, 29-30, 38-40, 56; major scale, 56

serial music: Alban Berg, 47, 57; Arnold Schoenberg, 47, 57, 58; Anton Webern, 47, 57; *see also* 12-tone system

single notes, 37

staccato, 5, 26

tango: *see* dance

tape, in musique-concrete, 59

teacher-student dialogues, 4, 6-7, 11-13, 15-19, 25-27, 29-30, 31-34, 35-37, 38-40, 48-50, 51-54, 55, 58-59

telephone conversation as dialogue technique, 21

tempo, 6, 20

tetrachords, 39

timbre, 26, 49

tone clusters, 21

tones, 21, 39-40

triads, 37-38

12-tone row: *see* 12-tone system

12-tone system, 56, 58-59

waltz bass: *see* bass, waltz

9982